Heat

by Margie Burton, Cathy French, and Tammy Jones

Heat is all around us.

You cannot see it, but you can feel it.
Heat makes things feel warm.

Does heat make you feel better
when it is cold outside?

The sun gives us most of our heat.

Many things would die
without the heat from the sun.

Many things can give us heat.

Wood can give us heat.

Gas can give
us heat, too.

Your body can even give you heat.
When you rub your hands together,
you are making heat.

Can you feel it?

We use heat to warm our homes.

We use heat to cook our food.

We use heat to warm our bodies.

These things change when they get warm

The ice cream melts.

The butter melts on the warm toast.

The snowman melts, too.

We cannot see heat,
but we can see how warm it is outside
by using a thermometer.

We can measure the temperature of the air.

We cannot see heat,

but we can see how warm we are

by using a thermometer.

We can measure
the temperature
of our bodies.

We cannot see heat,

but we can see how warm our food is

by using a thermometer.

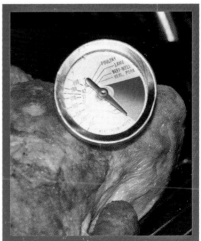

We can measure
the temperature
of our food.

We read some thermometers
by looking at the numbers.

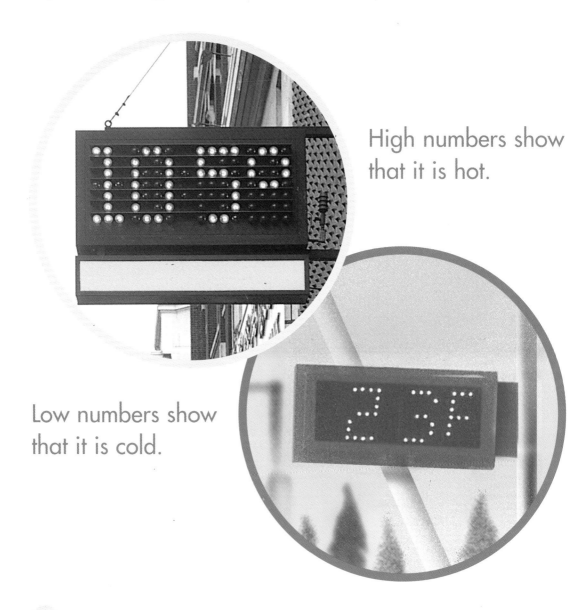

High numbers show
that it is hot.

Low numbers show
that it is cold.

We read some thermometers by looking at the red line.

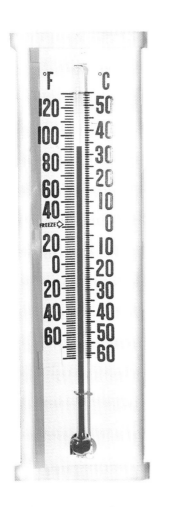

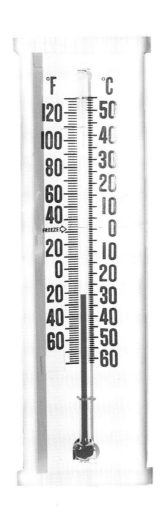

A long red line
shows that it is hot.

A short red line
shows that it is cold.

How do you use heat?